Collins

EXPLORERS

FASCINATING FACTS

D1471243

Published by Collins
An imprint of HarperCollins Publishers
Westerhill Road
Bishopbriggs
Glasgow G64 2QT
www.harpercollins.co.uk

First published 2016

A catalogue record for this book is available from the British Library

ISBN 978-0-00-816926-8

10 9 8 7 6 5 4

Printed in China by R R Donnelley APS Co Ltd.

All mapping in this book is generated from Collins Bartholomew digital databases.
Collins Bartholomew, the UK's leading independent geographical information supplier,
can provide a digital, custom, and premium mapping service to a variety of markets.
For further information:
Tel: +44 (0)208 307 4515
e-mail: collinsbartholomew@harpercollins.co.uk
Visit our website at: www.collins.co.uk   www.collinsbartholomew.com

If you would like to comment on any aspect of this book, please contact us at the
above address or online.
e-mail: collinsmaps@harpercollins.co.uk

MIX
Paper from
responsible sources
FSC™ C007454
www.fsc.org

Contents

Introduction

The thrill of exploring draws each one of us in at a young age, and the same was true for many of the explorers in this book. As far back as 1271, when the 17-year-old Marco Polo started out on a life of exploration to today's teenagers like Jordan Romero, the spirit of adventure lies within all of us.

This book looks at some of the greatest explorers of all time, as they opened up the world in which they lived, discovering new rivers, countries and continents, finding new routes, and meeting new challenges. These were explorations which took place at sea, in deserts, on mountains, and in space, from places with the hottest temperatures ever recorded to regions which have the coldest temperatures in the world.

The difficulties these explorers faced are difficult to imagine in modern times – lack of equipment, little information, illness and disease, prejudice against women, attacks by people and animals, and the ever-present threat of starvation and exhaustion. Yet, these brave men and women continued in spite of the challenges to make the history that shaped the world we live in today.

So much of the world and beyond has been explored over the last few centuries and yet there are some places on Earth still to

Explorers timeline

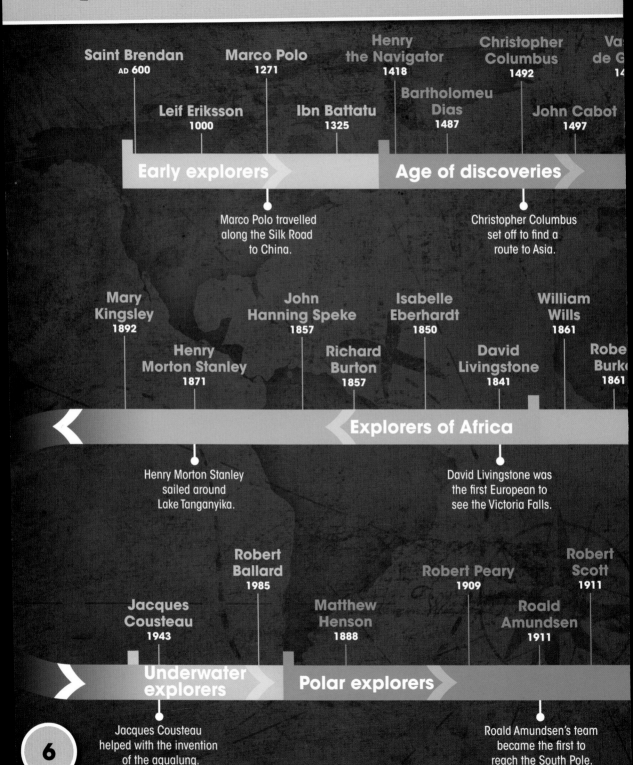

Saint Brendan
AD 600

Leif Eriksson
1000

Marco Polo
1271

Ibn Battatu
1325

Henry the Navigator
1418

Bartholomeu Dias
1487

Christopher Columbus
1492

John Cabot
1497

Va: de G
14

Early explorers

Age of discoveries

Marco Polo travelled along the Silk Road to China.

Christopher Columbus set off to find a route to Asia.

Mary Kingsley
1892

Henry Morton Stanley
1871

John Hanning Speke
1857

Richard Burton
1857

Isabelle Eberhardt
1850

David Livingstone
1841

William Wills
1861

Robe Burk
1861

Explorers of Africa

Henry Morton Stanley sailed around Lake Tanganyika.

David Livingstone was the first European to see the Victoria Falls.

Robert Ballard
1985

Jacques Cousteau
1943

Matthew Henson
1888

Robert Peary
1909

Roald Amundsen
1911

Robert Scott
1911

Underwater explorers

Polar explorers

Jacques Cousteau helped with the invention of the aqualung.

Roald Amundsen's team became the first to reach the South Pole.

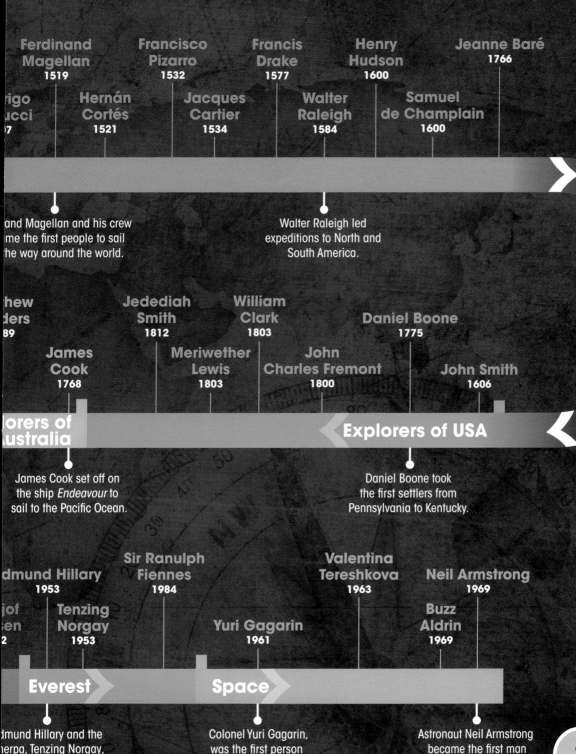

Ferdinand Magellan 1519

Francisco Pizarro 1532

Francis Drake 1577

Henry Hudson 1600

Jeanne Baré 1766

...igo ...ucci ...7

Hernán Cortés 1521

Jacques Cartier 1534

Walter Raleigh 1584

Samuel de Champlain 1600

...and Magellan and his crew ...me the first people to sail ...he way around the world.

Walter Raleigh led expeditions to North and South America.

...hew ...ers ...89

Jedediah Smith 1812

William Clark 1803

Daniel Boone 1775

James Cook 1768

Meriwether Lewis 1803

John Charles Fremont 1800

John Smith 1606

...lorers of ...ustralia

Explorers of USA

James Cook set off on the ship *Endeavour* to sail to the Pacific Ocean.

Daniel Boone took the first settlers from Pennsylvania to Kentucky.

Sir Ranulph Fiennes 1984

Valentina Tereshkova 1963

Neil Armstrong 1969

...dmund Hillary 1953

Buzz Aldrin 1969

...jof ...en ...2

Tenzing Norgay 1953

Yuri Gagarin 1961

Everest

Space

...dmund Hillary and the ...herpa, Tenzing Norgay, ...ere the first to reach the summit.

Colonel Yuri Gagarin, was the first person in space.

Astronaut Neil Armstrong became the first man to step on the moon.

Early explorers

Leif Eriksson

Saint Brendan

Ibn Battuta

Marco Polo

GREENLA

NEWFOUNDL

NORTH
AMERICA

ATLANTIC
OCEAN

ICELAND

Tralee

EUROPE

Venice

Istanbul

Tangier

Marrakesh

Damascus

Cairo

Mecca

Timbuktu

AFRICA

Mogadishu

Mombasa

Kilwa

ASIA

Beijing

Delhi

Chittagong

Surat

Calicut

INDIAN OCEAN

ERIKSSON
BRENDAN
BATTUTA
POLO

Leif Eriksson

Son of the famous Viking 'Erik the Red', Leif Eriksson was the first European known to sail to America. Leaving Greenland in around AD 1000, he sailed first to Canada and then on to 'Vinland', or Newfoundland. His nickname ('the Lucky') came from his success in trading wood on his journey.

Leif Eriksson sailed in a Viking longship – a sturdy wooden boat with the warriors' shields hung over the sides.

Saint Brendan

Saint Brendan 'the Bold' was a 6th-century Irish monk who made many dangerous sea voyages in the Atlantic Ocean, possibly sailing as far as North America. His tales describe him seeing 'floating ice palaces' and coming across a giant sea monster.

Ibn Battuta

One of the earliest explorers was the Moroccan Muslim, Muhammad Ibn Battuta, who set off on a pilgrimage (or 'hajj') to Mecca in 1325 at the age of 21. Thirty years later he had travelled around 120 000 km (75 000 miles) through various countries of the world.

Greatest traveller of his time

During his travels, Ibn Battuta explored many countries including Egypt, Syria, Peria, Arabia, India, China, and parts of Africa. Some people could not believe that one person could go to so many places, especially in those days, when travel was so difficult and dangerous. Ibn Battuta had many adventures on his travels, including being shipwrecked and getting married several times.

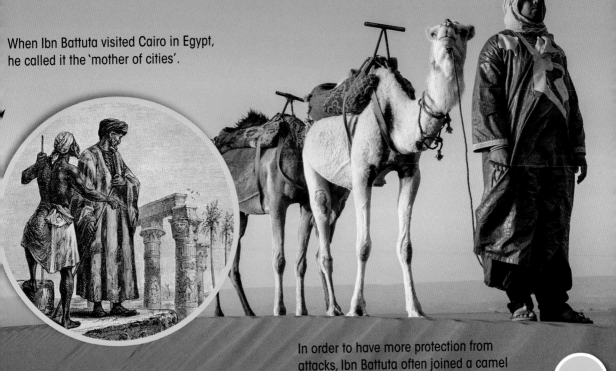

When Ibn Battuta visited Cairo in Egypt, he called it the 'mother of cities'.

In order to have more protection from attacks, Ibn Battuta often joined a camel caravan instead of travelling alone.

Marco Polo

In 1271, 17-year-old Marco Polo travelled over 6400 km (4000 miles) with his father and uncle from his native city of Venice in Italy along the Silk Road to China. It took four years for them to complete the journey, arriving in China in 1275.

The Silk Road

The Silk Road was a route used by traders to travel between Europe and China so that they could swap silks and spices for silver and horses. They travelled on foot or by horse or camel. The route was dangerous, not just because of the difficult terrain, but there were often robbers lying in wait to steal their goods.

Did you know?

The Gobi Desert ('Gobi' means 'waterless') is the fifth largest desert in the world and is getting bigger every year. Although you think of deserts as hot places, the temperature can drop to as low as -40 °C, which is the same temperature as at the North Pole in winter!

The Silk Road crossed through deserts and mountain ranges.

There is a monument to Marco Polo in Ulan Bator in Mongolia.

Travels around China

Marco Polo spent many years working in China for the Mongolian ruler Kublai Khan. While he was there he learned to speak four languages and became very rich. By the time he left in 1295, he had travelled over 24 000 km (15 000 miles). The journey back to Venice took two years by sea. Of the 600 passengers and crew that left China on the return voyage, only 18 were alive at the end.

Il Milione

Marco Polo was captured in 1298 during a sea battle and spent time in prison. While he was there he told another prisoner about his travels and these stories were made into a book called 'Il Milione', which is known in English as 'The Travels of Marco Polo'. This book inspired future explorers such as Christopher Columbus.

Age of discoveries

Henry the Navigator

Bartholomeu Dias

John Cabot

Vasco de Gama

Christopher Columbus

Amerigo Vespucci

Hernán Cortés

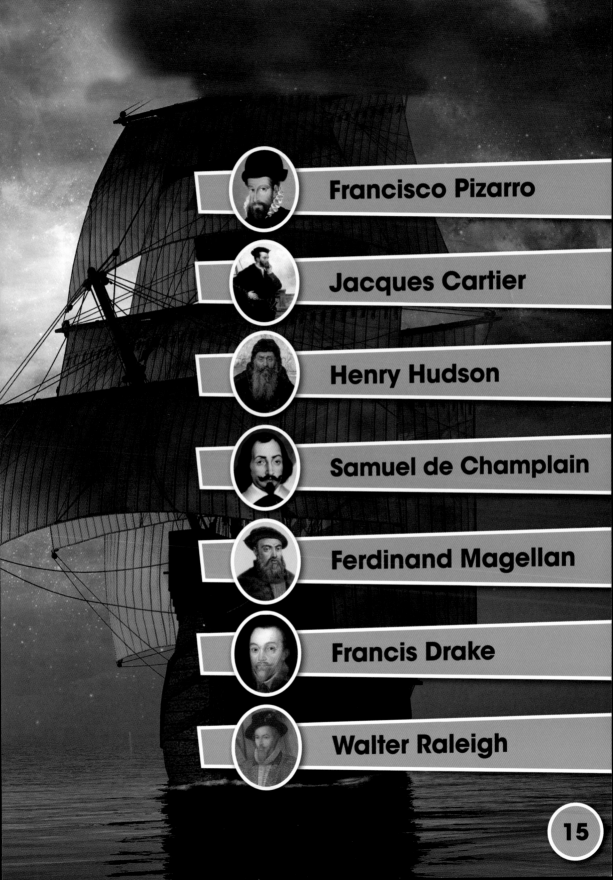

Francisco Pizarro

Jacques Cartier

Henry Hudson

Samuel de Champlain

Ferdinand Magellan

Francis Drake

Walter Raleigh

GREENLAND

NORTH
AMERICA

Quebec

New York

Los Angeles

Honolulu

Mexico
City

PACIFIC
OCEAN

Panama City

Quito

SOUTH
AMERICA

Lima

Cusco

ATLANTIC
OCEAN

Rio de
Janeiro

Valparaiso

Buenos Aires

San
Julián

Pl

— HENRY	— PIZARRO
— DIAS	— CARTIER
— CABOT	— HUDSON
— DA GAMA	— CHAMPLAIN
— COLUMBUS	— MAGELLAN
— VESPUCCI	— DRAKE
— CORTÉS	— RALEIGH

ARCTIC OCEAN

~~ROPE~~

A S I A

PACIFIC
OCEAN

~~RICA~~

Calicut

Mogadishu

Malindi

INDIAN
OCEAN

OCEANIA

Cape
Town

SOUTHERN OCEAN

A N T A R C T I C A

Henry the Navigator

In spite of his name, Henry the Navigator was not really a navigator or an explorer at all but a Portuguese prince. However, Henry paid for other sailors to carry out expeditions to explore the coast of Africa and started off the Great Age of Discovery in the early 15th century.

School of navigation

One of Prince Henry's greatest achievements was to start up a school of navigation in 1418. Here sailors were taught the skills they needed to explore the rough oceans, such as the dreaded 'Sea of Darkness'. Henry himself used his mapping skills to create charts of the areas explored, in particular the West African coast.

In around 1420, Henry the Navigator's sailors discovered the island of Porto Santo. They put the first rabbits on the island which unfortunately then ate everything!

The Discovery Monument in Lisbon, Portugal, commemorates all the explorers from the Great Age of Discovery.

Bartholomeu Dias

Bartholomeu Dias was a Portuguese explorer in the Great Age of Discovery. In 1487, he was the first European to sail round the Cape of Good Hope at the southern tip of Africa. His success created trading routes between Europe and Asia, the land of spices.

Challenges at sea

Life at sea was very hard for sailors in the 15th and 16th centuries. Supplies of food and water were limited, which led to starvation. Rats on board ships and a lack of fresh fruit meant that illness and disease were common. Storms at sea caused men to fall overboard and drown. And, of course, there was also the danger of a pirate attack!

It is thought that the Cape of Good Hope was originally called the Cape of Storms.

It was on an expedition in 1500 that Bartholomeu Dias's ship was hit by a storm and sank. The great explorer was lost at sea.

John Cabot

Although he was born in Italy, John Cabot (or Giovanni Caboto, as he is known in Italian), came to live in England in 1495. He only stayed for two years; in 1497 he set off in his small boat, the *Matthew*, to find a route to Asia by sea.

A statue has been erected to John Cabot in Newfoundland.

St John's in Newfoundland is the oldest city in North America.

The king's money

It cost a lot of money to fit out a ship which cou travel across the oceans and to pay the crew to sail it. John Cabot, like many explorers, had to ask for money from the monarch (in this case King Henry VII). Monarchs would fund explore in the hope that they would get rich when the explorer returned!

An Englishman in Canada

John Cabot, however, did not find his way to Asia and instead he landed in Newfoundland, off the coast of Canada. He was the first European to do so since the Viking, Leif Eriksson Cabot explored the Canadian coastline and claimed that part of Canada as belonging to the British.

Vasco de Gama

With the Silk Road across land to Asia becoming more difficult and dangerous, it was important that a trade route was found by sea between Europe and Asia. The Portuguese explorer Vasco de Gama sailed from Portugal (Europe) in 1497 and finally arrived in India (Asia) in May, 1498. He had done it!

Admiral of the Ocean

As the first European explorer to sail around Africa to Asia, Vasco de Gama then made sure that Portugal controlled all trade with India. When he returned to Portugal he was greeted as a hero and given the title 'Admiral of the Ocean'. On future trips he brought back treasure and spices and in 1519 he was made a Portuguese count.

It is said that Vasco de Gama could be a violent and cruel man. On one of his expeditions he is believed to have destroyed a fleet of Arab ships and killed the crews. This was not a good way for the Europeans to start trading with India.

Spices were what Europeans wanted to trade for.

Christopher Columbus

Born in Italy in 1451, Christopher Columbus was so inspired by Marco Polo's book about his travels to Asia that he decided he also wanted to find a route to Asia by sea. In 1492, using money given by the King and Queen of Spain, he set off on a voyage that would make history.

Is this Asia?

Christopher Columbus and his crew set off with three boats, including the *Santa Maria*, captained by Columbus. On 12th October 1492 they had their first sight of land. Columbus was sure he had reached Asia, but he had in fact sailed as far as the Bahamas. On his next expeditions, he also landed at Cuba, the Dominican Republic, and Venezuela. His discovery of this New World started the rush by Europeans to settle in North America.

When Christopher Columbus first landed at San Salvador (an island in The Bahamas), he called the native peoples 'Indians' as he was so sure he had reached Asia, or 'the Indies' as it was then called.
............................➤

Unwelcome guests

Unfortunately the European sailors didn't always behave very well in the places they landed. They got into fights with the local people and were caught looting and stealing gold. In addition, the Europeans brought with them diseases which killed many of the Native American peoples.

▲ Until he died, Christopher Columbus believed that he had found a new route to Asia.

Santa Maria ran aground off the coast Hispaniola, the second largest island in Caribbean. Luckily the friendly local chief t men out to rescue the crew.

Columbus Day was intended to celebrate the links between North America and Europe.

Many parts of North America celebrate the history and culture of Native Americans.

Celebrations

Many parts of North America celebrate Columbus Day on the second Monday in October. However, a lot of people believe that this is unfair to Native Americans, many of whom suffered and died as a result of the European settlers. It is becoming more common to celebrate Indigenous Peoples Day throughout America.

Amerigo Vespucci

It was another Italian explorer, Amerigo Vespucci, who, while sailing along the coast of South America, realised that the Americas were not part of Asia. In 1507, the first map showing this discovery gave the New World the name of 'America' in his honour.

Early maps

Until this time, European explorers had seen the world as divided into only three continents — Europe, Asia, and Africa. After Amerigo Vespucci's travels, maps showed another continent separated by a large ocean, now called the Pacific Ocean.

In 1500, Vespucci discovered the mouth of the Orinoco River in Venezuela.

A map from 1507 showing 'America'

Hernán Cortés

Called a conquistador (conqueror), Hernán Cortés was a cruel and ruthless Spanish explorer who was sent to Mexico in 1521. Over the next two years he killed thousands of Aztec Mexicans, took their land, and robbed them. He became the ruler of Mexico until 1524 when he had to retire.

Francisco Pizarro

Another Spanish conquistador, Francisco Pizarro, showed the same cruelty in Peru. In 1532, with only a small army, he tricked and then killed the Inca emperor and conquered the Inca empire.

The famous Inca city of Machu Picchu in Peru was abandoned after the Spanish invasion, and was only discovered again in 1911.

Jacques Cartier

The French explorer Jacques Cartier led expeditions into inland Canada between 1534 and 1541. He was looking for gold, paddling around 1000 km (625 miles) along the St Lawrence River. He named the region he explored 'Kanata', which means Canada in the Huron-Iroquois language. Unfortunately for him, he never did find gold.

Jacques Cartier tried to set up a settlement in Quebec, but it was Samuel de Champlain who succeeded in 1608. Today Quebec is one of Canada's largest and most important cities.

Henry Hudson

Henry Hudson was an English explorer who carried out a number of voyages around 1600 to try to find a way through the ice in the Arctic Ocean. Although he was not successful in this, he did make some important discoveries, including a harbour which would later become New York City.

Hudson Bay and the Hudson River in Canada were both named after Henry Hudson.

Samuel de Champlain

Another French explorer, Samuel de Champlain, made several expeditions by canoe up the St Lawrence River. He wanted to explore inland Canada and to set up a fur-trading centre. He made friends with the local Huron Indians, who helped him along the way. Samuel de Champlain became known as the 'Father of Canada'.

The fur trade

The fur trade was started by local people who swapped furs for tools and weapons. As French and British settlers came to Canada, they started to take control of fur trading. Over the next hundred years or so, thousands of animals were killed for their fur and this had a big impact on the animal population at the time.

In order to move easily across the country, traders travelled along rivers by canoe.

One of the longest rivers in North America, the St Lawrence River stretches from the Atlantic Ocean to the Great Lakes. In winter it can freeze over in parts, which made life difficult for early explorers.

Ferdinand Magellan

The Portuguese explorer Ferdinand Magellan left Spain in 1519 with five ships and over 250 men. Three years later only 18 of those men returned to Spain, but they had become the first people to sail all the way around the world!

An epic voyage

Going against what people at the time believed was possible, Ferdinand Magellan and his crews sailed west around South America and then across the 'Sea of the South' or the Pacific Ocean. Apart from the expected difficulties of bad weather and lack of food (at one point the men had to eat sawdust), Ferdinand Magellan also had to deal with a mutiny from two of his ships' captains. He had the captains executed for their lack of loyalty.

The *Victoria* was the only ship from Magellan's fleet to make the full voyage.

Magellanic penguins are named after the explorer, who was the first person to see them.

Unfortunately Ferdinand Magellan himself was killed during a fight in the Philippines and did not actually make the full voyage around the world. However, his voyage proved once and for all that the world was round!

The Strait of Magell joins the Atlantic an Pacific Oceans.

The first woman to sail around the world was Jeanne Baré between 1766 and 1769. As the French at the time did not allow women on their ships, she had to disguise herself as a man and call herself Jean Baret.

e first plane Amelia Earhart ught was a yellow biplane.

Amelia Earhart and Fred Noonan in Puerto Rico during their attempt to fly around the world.

Record solo flight

aving set her first flying record in 1921, melia Earhart became the first woman to y solo across the Atlantic Ocean in 1932. ve years later, Earhart and her companion red Noonan attempted to fly around the orld. Unfortunately, before they were able o complete their journey, the plane and its ilots mysteriously disappeared.

Around the world by bike

The first woman to cycle around the world was Annie Londonderry (she had changed her name from Kopchovsky). In 1894, she set off from Boston, America, with a change of clothes and a revolver, leaving her husband and three young children. Fifteen months later she returned as a celebrity!

At 16 years old, Laura Dekker is the youngest person to sail around the world.

Francis Drake

Between 1577 and 1580, the Englishman Francis Drake led the second expedition around the world in his ship, the *Golden Hind*. Not really an explorer, Francis Drake was a privateer who had been sent by his country to carry out sea raids. Drake and his crew looted Spanish ships for their silver and gold to bring back to England.

A replica of Francis Drake's ship, the *Golden Hind*, can be seen in London.

Fame and fortun

Having brought back a huge amount of treasure for himself and his country, Queen Elizabeth knighted him and he became Sir Francis Drake. Not only very rich he also became one of the most famous men of Elizabethan time

The Spanish Armada

In 1588 the King of Spain sent a fleet of Spanish ships called the Spanish Armada to fight the English ships. Sir Francis Drake helped to defeat the Spanish an the English navy became the m powerful navy in the world.

The Spanish called Sir Francis Drake 'El Draque', which means 'The Dragon' in English.

Walter Raleigh

Walter Raleigh led expeditions to North and South America to build up trade, found settlements, and search for El Dorado (the land of gold). Between 1584 and 1589 he helped to found a colony in North America, which he called Virginia. Many believe that he first brought the potato to Britain from America!

▲ Walter Raleigh watches as his new discovery, potatoes, are planted in Britain.

A traitor's end

Walter Raleigh was arrested for treason against King James I and held for 13 years in the Tower of London. The day before he was due to die, he was released. But in 1618 he was imprisoned again and this time he was beheaded. It is said that his wife was given his head and that she kept it until she died, 29 years later.

▲ The Tower of London is where Walter Raleigh was held between 1604 and 1617.

31

Explorers of USA

Meriwether Lewis

William Clark

Daniel Boone

Jedediah Smith

John Smith

John Charles Fremont

HUDSON
BAY

CANADA

ROCKY MOUNTAINS

Great
Falls

Fort Mandan

South
Pass

Council
Bluffs

Salt Lake
City

ort
op

nento

New York

APPALACHIAN MOUNTAINS

Washington

St Louis

Las Vegas

Westport

San Diego

UNITED STATES OF AMERICA

ATLANTIC
OCEAN

ACIFIC
OCEAN

MEXICO

GULF OF
MEXICO

LEWIS & CLARK
BOONE
JOHN SMITH
JEDEDIAH SMITH
FREMONT

Meriwether Lewis and William Clark

In 1803 the American President, Thomas Jefferson, bought some land in Louisiana (southern USA) from the French and sent his secretary, Meriwether Lewis to explore it. Lewis was joined by his friend William Clark, and a number of others. Together they travelled by river and land to cover around 14 400 km (9000 miles) in just under two years.

Lewis and Clarke found that the easiest way to travel along the rivers was in a dugout canoe made from a hollowed out tree trunk.

York

Joining William Clark on the expedition was his African-American slave, York. Clark thought very highly of York and, once they had returned from their trip, he freed him from being a slave.

The explorers came across the grizzly bear for the first time on their travels.

Meriwether Lewis looks out to the Rocky Mountains.

Sacagawea

Sacagawea and her family were Native Americans who travelled with Lewis and Clarke's group. Sacagawea helped the explorers to find safe food to eat, and made medicines from plants, while her husband acted as a guide. She also translated for them when they met other Native American peoples. Having a woman and baby in the group made them seem less threatening.

The heroes return

The two men had to face many challenges while travelling, including fighting off wild animals, sailing down raging rivers, and crossing the high, snowy Rocky Mountains. When they returned, the two men were seen as heroes in America and were held in great honour by the US President.

A golden Sacagawea dollar coin was used in America in 2000.

Daniel Boone

Daniel Boone was an American wilderness explorer and hunter who found a way to take the first settlers across part of America from Pennsylvania to Kentucky. After the route opened in 1775, thousands of Americans used the so-called Wilderness Road, travelling on foot or horseback to find new places to settle.

The Wilderness Road crossed through the Appalachian Mountains.

Jedediah Smith

The first European American to cross the Rocky Mountains was the explorer and hunter Jedediah Smith in around 1812. During his travels, Smith was involved in fights with Native Americans, and was, in fact, killed during one of these fights at the age of 32.

Jedediah Smith also crossed the Great Basin Desert. Death Valley, in the Great Basin holds the record for the hottest temperature ever recorded: 134 °F in July 1913.

John Smith

In 1606 John Smith, an Englishman, sailed for America as one of around 100 settlers. He became one of the leaders of a new settlement, which was called Jamestown. The first few years there were very difficult and many of the settlers died from starvation and disease. John Smith ordered them to work to survive.

ocahontas

n Smith carried out several expeditions from Jamestown. On one of them he was tured by the Powhatan people, and the story is that his life was saved by 'Pocahontas', e chief's daughter. She was later captured and then married to another English settler, n Rolfe. She became one of the first Native Americans to visit Britain, in 1616.

John Charles Fremont

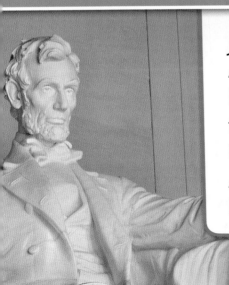

John Charles Fremont was another American explorer who became known by some as 'The Great Pathfinder' thanks to his exploration of the western United States. On one trip, he led American troops to fight for and win large parts of California from Mexico.

John Charles Fremont ran for President of the USA in 1856. He wanted to stop slavery. He didn't win, but in 1865, slavery was abolished under President Abraham Lincoln (left).

Explorers of Australia

James Cook

Matthew Flinders

Robert Burke

William Wills

T

Perth

INDIAN
OCEAN

SOUTHE

PACIFIC OCEAN

NEW
GUINEA

CORAL SEA

GREAT
BARRIER REEF

Townsville

USTRALIA

Adelaide

Sydney

Melbourne

TASMAN
SEA

Auckland

Wellington

Hobart

NEW
ZEALAND

TASMANIA

EAN

COOK
FLINDERS
BURKE & WILLS

39

James Cook

In 1768, the British astronomer and explorer James Cook set off in his ship *Endeavour* to sail to the Pacific Ocean. He wanted to study how the planet Venus passed in front of the Sun. The voyage took him to the islands we now know as New Zealand and then on to Australia.

Plant and animal life

One of the ship's passengers was a famous scientist called Joseph Banks who discovered many different kinds of plants on the trip. Cook, Banks and the crew had to deal with snakes, crocodiles, scorpions, and the odd platypus during their travels. They didn't have to look too far to find a goat though – they took one with them on the ship to provide milk!

The first kangaroos to be seen by European were described as 'large as a greyhound, o mouse colour and very swift'.

When *Endeavour* ran aground on the Great Barrier Reef, James Cook is said to have wrapped a sail around the bottom of the ship so that he could continue his voyage.

Further expeditions

Leaving in 1772, James Cook set off on a second voyage and he and his crew were the first to cross the Antarctic Circle. His ship sailed to within 2000 km (1250 miles) of the South Pole. After this voyage he returned to England in 1775. Unfortunately James Cook died on his third voyage when he was attacked by Hawaiian warriors as he tried to get back a ship that had been stolen by them.

▲ Throughout his voyages Cook tried to get his crew to eat fresh fruit and vegetables so that they stayed healthy. He made his men eat sauerkraut (German pickled cabbage).

n inland sea?

hile James Cook explored the coast of Australia, e English explorer, Charles Sturt, was very terested in finding out if there was a large sea the middle of Australia. In 1830, he led an pedition to follow the Murray River inland, but e never came across the sea he was looking for.

The Sturt Desert in Australia is named after the explorer Charles Sturt.

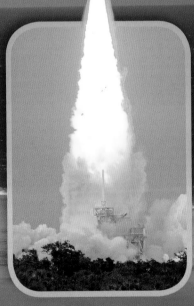

▲ NASA named their final space shuttle after James Cook's ship *Endeavour* from his first voyage.

Matthew Flinders

Matthew Flinders started out on his dream to become a sailor when he joined the Royal Navy in 1789 at the age of 15. Just nine years later, he and his companion George Bass proved that Tasmania was an island by sailing right round it. They explored part of the Australian coast in an 8-foot (2.5 m) boat called *Tom Thumb*!

Matthew Flinders was inspired by Daniel Defoe's boo 'Robinson Crusoe'

All around Australia

In 1801 Matthew Flinders was the captain of *Investigator*, which was the first ship to sail all the way around Australia. Flinders managed to complete this voyage in two years, in spite of illness, attacks on his crew and even a leaking ship. In 1824, 10 years after Flinders' death, Australia officially took on the name Flinders had given it.

A mysterious disappearance

In 1848, the explorer Ludwig Leichhardt went missing while studying nature in the Australian outback. As well as the explorer himself, all of his men, horses, and animals also vanished. Their disappearance is still a mystery!

The part of the Australia outback where Leichhar and his party disappeare is one of the most remo areas in Australia.

Robert Burke and William Wills

Burke and Wills were stopped from actually seeing the ocean by thick mangrove swamps.

In 1861, Robert Burke and William Wills set out to cross Australia from south to north in a bid to win a reward offered by the Australian government. Lack of experience, bad timing, and heavy rain made their trip very difficult. However, they did get to the mouth of the Flinders River on the north coast, becoming the first Europeans to do so.

After setting out on the return journey, Robert Burke and William Wills realised that they only had enough supplies for about half of the journey. Although helped by Aborigines, Burke and Wills became weaker and weaker until they died one after the other from starvation and exhaustion.

In 1862, a memorial was built in Castlemaine, Australia, to remember Robert Burke, William Wills and the other members of their party who died.

Explorers of Africa

Richard Burton

John Hanning Speke

Isabelle Eberhardt

Mary Kingsley

David Livingstone

Henry Morton Stanley

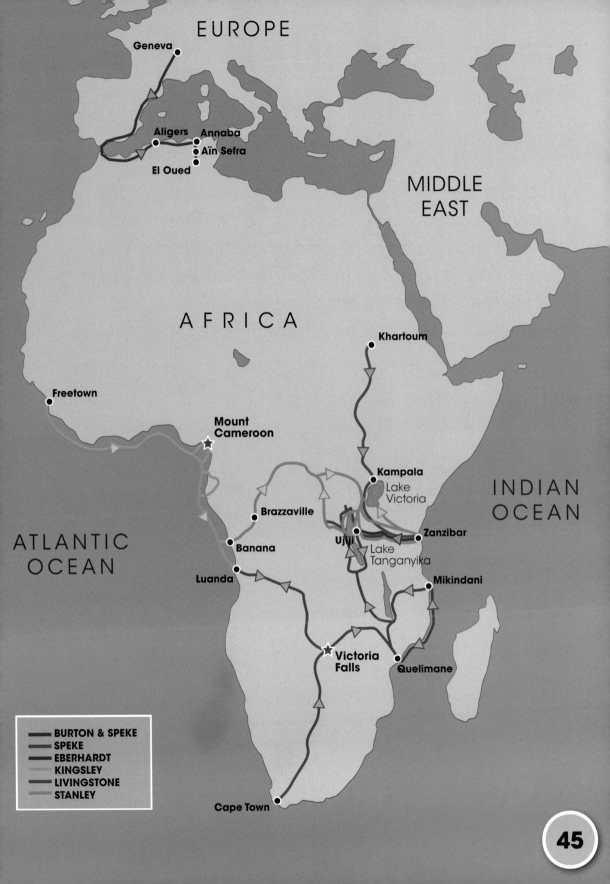

EUROPE

Geneva

MIDDLE
EAST

Aligers
Annaba
Aïn Sefra
El Oued

AFRICA

Khartoum

Freetown

Mount
Cameroon

Kampala
Lake
Victoria

INDIAN
OCEAN

Brazzaville

Zanzibar

Ujiji
Lake
Tanganyika

ATLANTIC
OCEAN

Banana

Mikindani

Luanda

Victoria
Falls

Quelimane

BURTON & SPEKE
SPEKE
EBERHARDT
KINGSLEY
LIVINGSTONE
STANLEY

Cape Town

45

Richard Burton and John Hanning Speke

Europeans knew very little about Africa until the 19th century. The landscape of deserts and rainforests made it difficult to explore and there was great danger from diseases such as malaria. In 1857, Richard Burton and John Hanning Speke set out to explore the River Nile and were the first Europeans to reach Lake Tanganyika.

Source of the River Nile

While Burton was ill with malaria, Speke continued to explore further along the river and made it as far as the biggest lake in Africa, which he named Lake Victoria. He claimed that he had found where the River Nile began, but Burton didn't agree. The men fell out over this and their friendship never recovered.

While at Lake Tanganyika, John Hanning Speke went deaf for a short while after he had to remove a beetle from his ear with a knife!

Richard Burton was a very clever man. He translated the book 'One Thousand and One Nights' into English, including the story of Aladdin.

Isabelle Eberhardt

Two hundred years ago it was difficult for women to travel, especially alone. The Swiss explorer and writer Isabelle Eberhardt had to disguise herself as a man in order to explore parts of the African desert. She learned to speak many languages, and wrote books about her adventures, but even had to publish some of these under a male name.

Isabelle Eberhardt made her home in West African country of Algeria.

Mary Kingsley

Mary Kingsley climbed Mount Cameroon, the est mountain in West Africa.

In 1892 the Englishwoman Mary Kingsley sailed to Africa to study nature and religion. She wrote about her adventures and was not afraid to speak out about the slave trade. Her belief was that all people were equal and deserved respect.

David Livingstone

The Scottish explorer David Livingstone was the first European to see the Victoria Falls, naming them after the British Queen Victoria. He went to Africa in 1841 as a doctor and to teach about Christianity, and also spent his time exploring the Zambezi River and the Kalahari Desert.

Loved by all

David Livingstone was very well liked and respected by the local African people as well as his African servants. In fact, one local teacher saved him when he was attacked by a lion. Throughout his life, he spoke out against the slave trade. When Livingstone died, his servants carried his body over 1400 km (900) miles across Africa so that he could be returned to Britian. His heart, however, was buried in Africa.

David Livingstone is buried in Westminster Abbey in London.

Did you know?
Locals call the Victoria Falls 'Mosi-oa-Tunya' which means 'Smoke that Thunders'.

Henry Morton Stanley

Sent by the *New York Herald* in 1871 to track down David Livingstone in Africa, Welshman Henry Morton Stanley (born as John Rowlands) found him eight months later in a small African village. Together the two great explorers sailed around Lake Tanganyika, before Stanley returned to Britain.

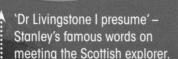

'Dr Livingstone I presume' – Stanley's famous words on meeting the Scottish explorer.

Hooked

After David Livingstone died, Henry Stanley was hooked on exploring and decided to return to Africa. He travelled around 1600 km (1000 miles) along the Congo River to the Atlantic Ocean. Funded by the Belgian king, he employed people to build roads through the Congo, but was said to have treated the African workers with some cruelty.

'The Scramble for Africa'

David Livingstone and Henry Morton Stanley were just two of the explorers involved in the race between countries (especially Britain, Portugal, and France) to claim land in Africa. One of the main reasons for doing this was to put an end to the slave trade, something that David Livingstone felt very strongly about.

Over a period of around 300 years, Europeans are said to have taken approximately 11 million people away from West Africa on ships to make them slaves.

Underwater explorers

Jacques Cousteau

Robert Ballard

Jacques Cousteau

Thanks to Jacques Cousteau and Emile Gagnan's invention of aqualung (a piece of diving equipment that helps divers breat underwater) in 1943, the French explorer and inventor was ab to research plant and animal species in the ocean. He made films and TV series about his work to teach people more abou ocean life and to make them aware of environmental problem

Divers can stay underwater for long periods with the proper equipment.

Fabien Cousteau, Jac Cousteau's' grandsor is passionate about t protection of sharks.

Keeping it in the family

Jacques Cousteau's children and grandchildren have carried on his love o the ocean – his grandson was diving from the age of four. Many member of the Cousteau family work together to help people understand how the can act responsibly and protect the oceans for future generations.

Robert Ballard

In 1985, the American underwater explorer Robert Ballard discovered the wreck of *Titanic*, which had hit an iceberg and sunk in 1912. Using a submersible (a type of submarine), he got the first photos of the famous ship where it lay over 3.5 km (2.25 miles) below the surface of the ocean.

Over 1500 people died when *Titanic* sank on her maiden voyage from the UK to America.

The JASON project

Robert Ballard wanted to help others to experience underwater exploration and so he set up the JASON project. His special underwater vehicle (called *Jason* after the Greek hero) explores under the sea and sends back live pictures and videos for people to watch around the world.

Highest and deepest points on Earth

Mount Everest 8484 m above sea level

⊛ **Location** Himalayas, China and Nepal

Mariana Trench 10 911 m below sea level

⊛ **Location** western Pacific Ocean

In 2012, James Cameron dived down to the Mariana Trench, the very deepest part of the ocean, which is nearly 11 km (6.5 miles) deep. While down there in his submersible, the *Deepsea Challenger*, he tweeted 'Can't wait to share what I'm seeing w/ you.'

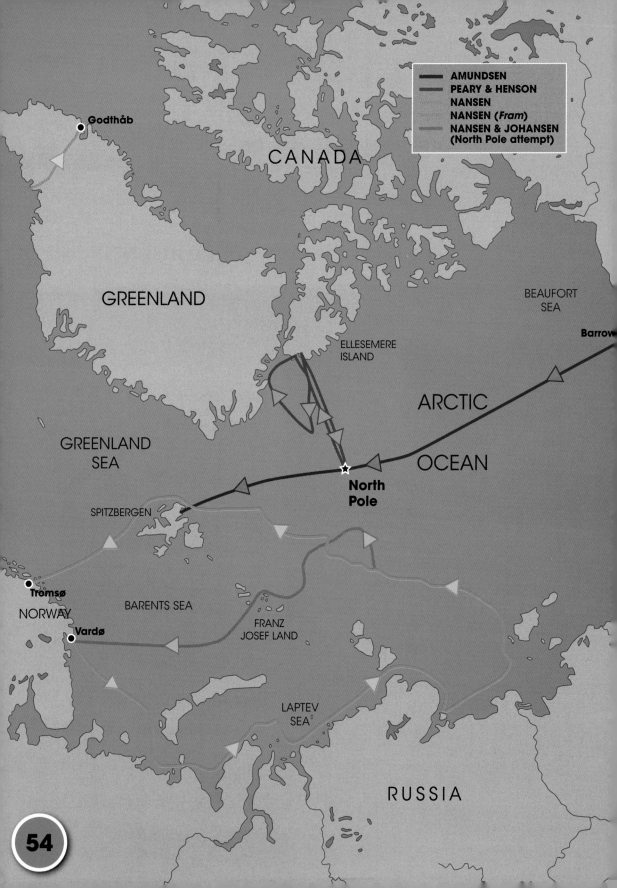

AMUNDSEN
PEARY & HENSON
NANSEN
NANSEN (*Fram*)
NANSEN & JOHANSEN
(North Pole attempt)

Godthåb

CANADA

GREENLAND

BEAUFORT
SEA

ELLESEMERE
ISLAND

ARCTIC

Barrow

GREENLAND
SEA

OCEAN

SPITZBERGEN

North
Pole

Tromsø

BARENTS SEA

NORWAY

Vardø

FRANZ
JOSEF LAND

LAPTEV
SEA

RUSSIA

Polar explorers

 Robert Peary

 **Matthew Henson**

 Fridtjof Nansen

 Roald Amundsen

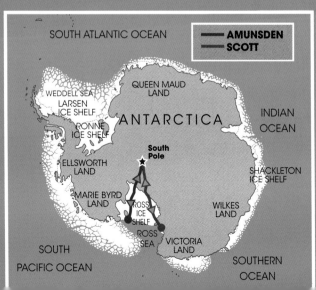 **Robert Scott**

— **AMUNSDEN**
— **SCOTT**

SOUTH ATLANTIC OCEAN

QUEEN MAUD LAND

WEDDELL SEA

LARSEN ICE SHELF

RONNE ICE SHELF

ANTARCTICA

INDIAN OCEAN

South Pole

ELLSWORTH LAND

SHACKLETON ICE SHELF

MARIE BYRD LAND

ROSS ICE SHELF

ROSS SEA

WILKES LAND

VICTORIA LAND

SOUTH PACIFIC OCEAN

SOUTHERN OCEAN

Robert Peary

In the race to be the first person to reach the North Pole, the American Robert Peary never gave up. In April 1909, on his eighth attempt, he at last achieved his dream, together with his travelling companion, Matthew Henson. In fact, nobody else travelled to the North Pole on foot for another 60 years!

Robert Peary suffered from frostbite because of the bitter cold in the Arctic regions and had to have eight toes amputated.

Matthew Henson

Matthew Henson was the first African-American Arctic explorer. He met Robert Peary in 1888 and was hired because of his excellent skills in Arctic exploration. After the pair reached the North Pole, Henson led the expedition back home.

Matthew Henson learned how to make igloos, drive dog sleds, and talk to the Inuit people in their own language. Without his skills, it would have been difficult for Peary to complete his expedition.

Fridtjof Nansen

The Norwegian explorer and scientist Fridtjof Nansen is celebrated as a hero, not only for his daring Arctic adventures, but also for his work in helping others. In 1922, Nansen was awarded the Nobel Peace Prize for the work that he did to help prisoners of war and refugees to return home.

North Pole attempt

Fridtjof Nansen made his name as the first person to ski across the ice cap in Greenland. He always had a passion for the Arctic region and in 1893 decided to follow the Arctic currents in his ship *Fram*. The ship and crew spent three years floating with the ice. During that time Nansen left the ship and attempted to walk to the North Pole and, although he came close to reaching it, unfortunately he was not successful.

The polar ship *Fram* was built to be sturdy and withstand the pressure of the ice crushing it.

In the Arctic region, there is at least one day a year when it is light all day and one day when it is completely dark. This is because of the way the Earth tilts. It is common to see the Aurora Borealis in this part of the world.

Roald Amundsen

The Norwegian explorer, Roald Amundsen, wanted to be the first person to reach the South Pole. His team set off in October 1911 and 99 days later, in December 1911, the Norwegians planted their flag at the South Pole. They beat the British team by 33 days!

Travelling across ice

Roald Amundsen and his team of explorers used husky dogs to help them travel across the ice more quickly. They also wrapped up in husky fur to keep warm, and when they ran out of food, they ate the dogs. While travelling to the South Pole, the Norwegians ate 22 of their dogs.

Sled dogs need to be strong, fast and have a lot of energy. They can reach speeds of around 30 kmph (19 mph).

Amundsen also liked to explore by air, flying over the North Pole in the 1920s. In 1928 he disappeared when his plane crashed over the Arctic Ocean.

Robert Scott

Robert Scott led a British team of explorers in the race to the South Pole. In 1911, after months of preparation, they set out and arrived in January 1912, 81 days later. To their huge disappointment, they found that the Norwegian team had reached the South Pole first!

Scott's diary

Robert Scott kept a diary of the expedition, writing about the difficulties the team faced on the way back. The team were hit by snowstorms and extremely low temperatures. One by one the men died until Scott and two others were trapped in their tents by a blizzard. Scott's entry in his diary reads 'It seems a pity, but I do not think I can write more.' Their frozen bodies were found in their tents later that year.

Captain Scott's diary gave people detailed information about his expedition to the South Pole.

Captain Oates

One of Scott's team, Captain Oates, showed great bravery during the expedition. The severe cold meant that he suffered from frostbite in his legs and feet so he couldn't walk very well. Knowing rations were low and that time was short, Oates told the team 'I'm going for a short walk, I may be some time.' He never returned.

Robert Scott's courage and that of his men made them heroes and there are a number of statues to him.

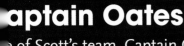
Captain Scott and his team of explorers reach the South Pole.

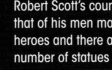

Everest

Sir Ranulph Fiennes

Edmund Hillary

Tenzing Norgay

Sir Ranulph Fiennes

In 1984, the English explorer Sir Ranulph Fiennes was called 'the world's greatest living explorer' by *The Guinness Book of Records*. Now he has led over 30 expeditions to explore many different parts of the world. In addition, he has raised millions of pounds for charity by completing various challenges, including seven marathons in seven days on seven continents in 2003.

An inspiring man

In 2015, Sir Ranulph became the oldest British person to take part in the 250 km (156 mile) 'Marathon des Sables' (known as 'the toughest footrace on earth') in the heat of the Sahara Desert. He has written many books about his experiences and continues to inspire many with his achievements.

Runners racing through the heat of the Sahara Desert in Morocco.

From pole to pole

Sir Ranulph Fiennes and Charles Burton were the first people to travel around the world on foot from pole to pole, covering around 83 685 km (52 000 miles). It took them three years in total. Luckily they had Ranulph Fiennes' dog, Bothie, with them to keep them company!

One of Sir Ranulph challenges was to climb Mount Everes aged 65.

Edmund Hillary and Tenzing Norgay

As the highest mountain in the world, Mount Everest has always been a target for climbers. In 1953, the New Zealand explorer Edmund Hillary and the Sherpa, Tenzing Norgay, were the first people to reach the summit, which is 8.5 km (5.5 miles) high. This is the height at which some planes fly!

he dangers of Mount Everest

here are a lot of dangers that need to be taken to account when climbing mountains as high as ose in the Himalayas. Apart from the danger of alanche, you can get snow blindness from the azzling snow, frostbite from the extreme cold, and titude sickness from the lack of oxygen at that eight. Over 200 people have died trying to climb ount Everest. Many of their bodies are still there.

Sherpas are local guides who know about the terrain, the weather, and the dangers of the climb. Without them it would be nearly impossible to climb Everest.

2010, 13-year-old Jordan omero climbed Mount Everest.

Space

Yuri Gagarin

Valentina Tereshkova

Neil Armstrong

Buzz Aldrin

Yuri Gagarin

The 'space race' was the name given to the contest to put the first person into orbit around the world. It was contested mainly between USA and Russia. Russian astronaut, Colonel Yuri Gagarin, made history as the first person in space. His spacecraft flew all the way around the Earth in 1961. The flight lasted 108 minutes and travelled at a speed of over 24 000 kmph (15 000 mph). Sadly, while training for his second trip into space, Gagarin died in a plane crash.

Before people went into space, animals, including fruit flies, dogs, and monkeys, were sent up in spaceships so that scientists could see the effects of space travel. Sadly, many did not survive the journey.

Valentina Tereshkova

Another Russian astronaut, Colonel Valentina Tereshkova, became the first woman to go into space. After 18 months of training, she spent three days in space, orbiting the Earth 48 times, and earning the title of 'Hero of the Soviet Union'.

The International Space Station (ISS) was launched in 1998 and allows all space agencies to work together to carry out research in space. Six astronauts, often from different countries, can live there at one time.

Neil Armstrong and Buzz Aldrin

On 20th July, 1969, American astronaut Neil Armstrong became the first man to step on the Moon, followed closely by Buzz Aldrin. A third member of the team, Michael Collins, kept the Lunar Module *Eagle* orbiting while the astronauts spent two hours on the Moon. Neil Armstrong even managed to take the first moon selfie!

'The *Eagle* has landed'

Over 600 million people across the world watched the Apollo 11 mission on television, when Neil Armstrong and Buzz Aldrin planted the American flag on the surface of the Moon. Unfortunately, as they left the Moon in the Lunar Module, the flag was blasted away by the force of the engines!

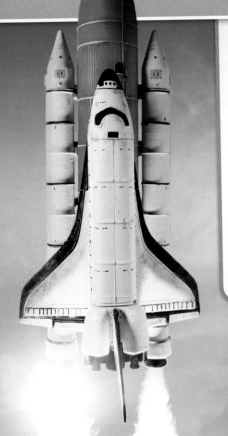

Space shuttles like this one made over 100 flights into space.

'That's one small step for man, one giant leap for mankind' – Neil Armstrong's famous first words on the Moon.

Useful words

astronaut a person who operates
a spacecraft

Aurora Borealis bands of glowing coloured
light sometimes seen in the sky in the Arctic

caravan a group of people and animals
travelling together, usually across a desert

challenge something that is new and
exciting, but requires a lot of effort

circumnavigate to sail, ride or fly all the
way round a place or country

conqueror a person who takes control of
another country by force

continent one of seven very large areas
of land in the world: Europe, North America,
South America, Africa, Asia, Antarctica,
Oceania

Elizabethan someone or something
that lived or was made during the reign
of Elizabeth I

expedition an organised journey made
for a special purpose, such as to explore

exploration travelling to and around
unknown places to find out more about them

fleet a group of ships travelling together

found to start or set up an organization
or settlement

frostbite the damage to your ears, fingers,
and toes caused by extreme cold

hajj the pilgrimage to Mecca that every
Muslim must make at least once in their life

indigenous someone or something that
comes from a particular country

invasion the act of entering a country or
territory by force

launch the act of sending a ship into water
or a rocket into space for the first time

looting the act of stealing goods, especially
in times of war

malaria a tropical disease which can be caused by the bite of mosquitoes

mutiny a rebellion against the captain or leader

Native American one of the indigenous peoples in America

navigate to travel safely across a stretch of water

orbit the curved path followed by an object going round a planet or the sun

outback the remote parts where very few people live in Australia

pilgrimage a journey to a holy place for religious reasons (also known as 'hajj')

plunder to steal things from a place, especially in times of war

privateer the captain of a ship who has been sent out by his country to rob other ships

route the road or path from one place to another

settler a person who starts to live in a new country

settlement a place where people have settled and built homes

slave trade the business of trading in slaves

space shuttle a spacecraft designed to be used for travelling into space

summit the highest point of a mountain

terrain a certain type of ground

trade the buying, selling or exchanging of different goods between people or companies

trader a person who buys, sells or exchanges different goods with others

treason the crime of betraying your country

voyage a long journey by sea or in space

Index

Acknowledgements

Publisher: Anne Mahon
Project Manager: Craig Balfour
Designer: Kevin Robbins
Layout: Craig Balfour, Gordon MacGilp
Text: Maree Airlie
Editorial: Lynne Tarvit, Jill Laidlaw

Photo credits

Cover images
Explorer: MP cz/Shutterstock.com
Map background: RTimages/Shutterstock.com
Magnifying glass compass: Tischenko Irina/Shutterstock.com
Davinf Livingstone: Public domain

t=top, c=centre, b=bottom, l=left, r=right   SS=Shutterstock

p1 MP cz/SS; **p2-3** Andrey_Kuzmin/SS; **p4-5** Anna Omelchenko/SS; **p6-7** Andrey_Kuzmin /SS; **p8** (top to bottom) public domain, MrCharco / CC BY-SA 3.0, public domain, public domain; **p10** Catmando/SS (t), Juancat/SS (b); **p11** public domain (l), The Visual Explorer / Shutterstock.com (r); **p12-13** Nithid/SS; **p12** Milosz_M/SS; **p13** alenvl / Shutterstock.com; **p14-15** Melkor3D/SS; **p14** (top to bottom) public domain, Biser Todorov/CC BY-SA 3.0, Skeezix1000/CC BY-SA 3.0, public domain, public domain, public domain, public domain; **p15** all explorer heads public domain; **p18** saiko3p /SS (t), CataFratto / SS (b); **p19** nodff/SS (t), Richard Cavalleri/SS (b); **p20** aiok/SS (t), Justek16/SS (b); **p21** Melkor3D/SS (t), Curioso (b); **p22-23** aldorado / Shutterstock.com; **p22** Everett Historical/SS; **p23** Paolo Bona / Shutterstock.com (t), Joseph Sohm / Shutterstock.com (c), Leonard Zhukovsky / Shutterstock.com (b); **p24** Janne Hamalainen/SS (b); **p25** DEA PICTURE LIBRARY/Getty Images (t), Jay Boucher/SS (b); **p26** Vlad G/SS (t), Joseph Sohm/SS (b); **p27** Maria Dryfhout/SS (t), pavels/SS (b); **p28** nbnserge / Shutterstock.com (r), Giedriius/SS (r); Tom Grundy/SS (b); **p29** Kletr/SS (t), Everett Historical/SS (c), Ukexpat/ CC BY-SA 3.0 (b); **p30** Alexandra Thompson / Shutterstock.com (l), Daniel Gale/SS (r); **p26** Universal History Archive / Getty Images (t); Salparadis/SS (b); **p32** all explorer heads public domain; **p34-35** Everett Historical/SS; **p34** photobar/SS (l), Scott E Read/SS (r); p35 Vladimir Wrangel/SS; **p36** Dave Allen Photography/ SS (t), tobkatrina/SS (b); **p37** public domain (t), Orhan Cam/ SS (b); **p38** (top to bottom) public domain, State Library of NSW/ CC BY-SA 3.0, public domain, public domain; **p40-41** Tomas Sykora/SS; **p40** Nick Fox/SS; p41 AS Food studio/SS (t), Jason and Bonnie Grower / Shutterstock.com (c), Janelle Lugge/ SS (b); **p42** Everett Historical/SS (t), Edward Haylan/SS (b); **p43** AustralianCamera/SS (t), Kim Britten / Shutterstock.com (b); **p44** all explorer heads public domain; **p46** Maciej Sojka/ SS (l), Tor Pur/SS (b); **p47** Ferderic B/SS (t), Michal Szymanski/ SS (b); **p48-49** Lynn Y/SS, **p48** Morphart Creation/SS (l), **p49** Stocksnapper/SS (t), Morphart Creation (b); **p50** Peters, Hans / Anefo/ CC BY-SA 3.0 (t), public domain (b); **p52** Sergiy Zavgorodny/SS (l), Stefan Pircher/SS (r); **p53** Everett Historical/ SS (l), best works/SS (r); **p55** all explorer heads public domain; **p56** Christopher Wood/SS (t), Smit/SS (b); **p57** Oleg Golovnev/ SS (t), Incredible Arctic/SS(b); **p58** prochasson/SS (t), George Burba/SS (b); **p59** public domain (t); BasPhoto/SS (c); public domain (b); **p60-61** Galyna Andrushko/SS; **p60** (top to bottom) David Ward/ CC BY-SA 3.0, public domain, public domain, **p62** PIERRE VERDY/Getty Images (t), Galyna Andrushko/SS (b); **p63** Zzvet / Shutterstock.com (t), Daniel Prudek/SS (b); **p64-65** Eric Meola/SS; **p64** (top to bottom) public domain, RIA Novosti archive, image #612748 / Alexander Mokletsov / CC-BY-SA 3.0, public domain, public domain, **P66** l i g h t p o e t/SS (t), Andrey Armyagov/SS (b); **p67** Fer Gregory/SS (t); public domain (b); **p68-72** Andrey_Kuzmin/SS